Be A Friend

The Story of African American Music in Song, Words and Pictures

Composed and written by Leotha Stanley

Illustrated by Henry Hawkins

Zino Press

Zino Press Children's Books
Middleton, Wisconsin

Special thanks to:

- The principals, teachers, and support staffs of the schools I visit. You made me feel comfortable.

- The music teachers, especially Julie Cowing, Renee Forrest, and Bev Haimerl. My school residencies would not have run as smoothly without your input and organizational skills.

- The thousands of students I've worked with since 1991. You have helped show me that we can learn to appreciate each other and work together regardless of our differences.

- My family who hasn't seen me much because of the many hats I wear. This project will allow my mission to continue while giving me more time to spend with those I love.

- Zino Press for recognizing the need for this boo its patience during production.

It's important to be a friend who cares. – *L. S.*

Zino Press Children's Books
A Division of Knowledge Unlimited, Inc.
2348 Pinehurst Drive
Middleton, WI 53562
800 356-2303

Music © 1994 by Musical-Lee Yours
Text © 1994 by Zino Press Children's Books
Illustrations © 1994 by Henry Hawkins
Edited by Judith Laitman
Designed by Henry Hawkins and Maggie Zoeller
Cover illustration by Henry Hawkins   Cover design by Patrick Ready
Photo research by Henry Hawkins and Paul Synnes
All rights reserved.
ISBN 1-55933-153-4
Printed in China
Through Palace Press International
San Francisco, California
First Zino Press printing, December 1994
This is printing number 10 9 8 7 6 5 4 3 2

Stanley, Leotha.
   Be a friend : the story of African American music in song, words, and
pictures / composed and written by Leotha Stanley ; illustrated by Henry
Hawkins.
         p.   cm.
   ISBN 1-55933-153-4 (pbk.) : $19.95
   1. Afro-Americans—Music—History and criticism—Juvenile literature.
2. Music—United States—History and criticism—Juvenile literature. [1.
Afro-Americans—Music—History and criticism. 2. Music—History and
criticism.] I. Hawkins, Henry
(Henry Philip). ill.
ML3556.S86 1994
780' .89'96073—dc20

                                                            94-29130
                                                            CIP
                                                            MN AC

Dear Friends,

While I was growing up in Milwaukee, Wisconsin, I heard African American music on the radio, on TV, in church, and at dances. There was jazz, gospel, blues, spirituals. There was rhythm and blues, soul, Motown, and rock and roll. When I liked a piece of music I would buy an album or a tape of it. The *music* was there for me, but no one told me where it came from. It was only later that I learned where African American music came from and how it has influenced all other kinds of American popular music.

At my elementary school in the 1960s, I was one of only four African Americans. But I was able to share my culture with my schoolmates. We talked about such things as hair, about music, and about dance. But we were not taught about the important contributions that African Americans had made to our way of life. And that frustrated me. That's why I want to tell this story about African American music and the history that helped shape it.

I wrote the original songs in this book for some of the same reasons that my ancestors wrote their music: to send a message and to express my feelings.

My message is that it's time now for us to come together. We all need to understand how much we share. Music is an important way to communicate with each other. Walls can be torn down, spirits can be lifted, and wounds can be healed. All through music.

That is the spirit of all African American music, and that is the spirit of this book.

Leotha Stanley
Madison, Wisconsin
August 1994

African Music —The Beginnings

We are almost a nation of dancers, musicians, and poets. Thus every great event . . . is celebrated in public dances which are accompanied with songs and music suited to the occasion.

Olaudah Equiano (1789),
one of the first Africans to write a book in English.

As far back as we can know, music was almost as much a part of African life as speaking. There was music when a person was born, and music when a person died. There was music for worship, and music to celebrate homecomings from war. There was happy music to welcome guests and to celebrate harvests of food. And, of course, there was music just for the joy of making music.

Telling stories musically was very important to Africans. Every village had its special musicians and poets who would pass on the history of the village in song. They would also sing praises about their leaders or special visitors. Sometimes they would just sing about their feelings. For Africans, music was a way to tell each other what they were thinking.

An 18th-century engraving of the city of Loango, near the mouth of the Congo River. African culture thrived on Africa's west coast, shown above.

One special way Africans "talked" with music was a style known as *call and response*. In call and response, a musician sings a line, then a group or chorus answers in some way. The chorus might repeat what the caller says, or they might sing something very different. As we'll see, call and response shows up in many types of African American music.

The Africans used many different types of instruments. Some of them were like harmonicas, fiddles, harps, and xylophones. Sometimes instruments were made to sound like human voices. This was another way to speak with music. But the most important instrument of all was the drum.

Drums were important in all kinds of ceremonies. Drums gave African music a strong rhythm and a lot of feeling and power. A drummer had to be a very good musician.

All of these things were important parts of African music. And because of some twists and turns of history, all of these and other African musical styles became important parts of American music.

Spirituals

Spirituals come from deep in the heart. They are often songs of pain. But they are also songs of hope. Spirituals come from a people who were sold into slavery, people who, even in their pain, made something beautiful.

These are examples of African art. Above is a bronze head from Benin. On the right is an Akan comb from Ghana. A game board from the Yoruba people is shown below.

Most of the people who planted the seeds of spirituals came to this country from different tribes and countries in West Africa.

These people had their own languages. They had their own cultures. They had their own families. And most important of all, they had their freedom.

Every possible inch of a ship's hold was used to carry slaves, as the picture above shows. Once they reached America, slaves were soon sold at auctions.

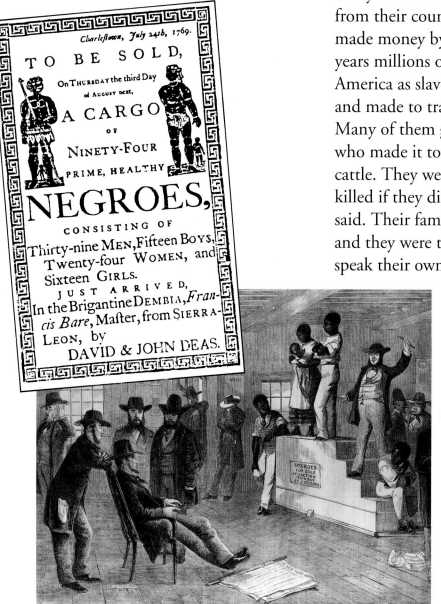

But starting in the 1600s and lasting into the 1800s, cruel and greedy people took many of these West African people away from their countries by force and then made money by selling them. Over the years millions of Africans were brought to America as slaves. They were put in chains and made to travel on crowded ships. Many of them got sick and died. Those who made it to America were sold like cattle. They were beaten and sometimes killed if they didn't do what their "owners" said. Their families were taken from them, and they were told that they couldn't speak their own languages anymore. They had no freedoms or rights the way other people did.

But these people did not lose their bravery and pride. And they did not give up their memories. This was especially true with their music. Music helped keep Africa alive in their hearts.

Many slaves fled the plantations
and escaped to the North.

$150 REWARD

RANAWAY from the subscriber, on the night of the 2d instant, a negro man, who calls himself *Henry May*, about 22 years old, 5 feet 6 or 8 inches high, ordinary color, rather chunky built, bushy head, and has it divided mostly on one side, and keeps it very nicely combed; has been raised in the house, and is a first rate dining-room servant, and was in a tavern in Louisville for 18 months. I expect he is now in Louisville trying to make his escape to a free state, (in all probability to Cincinnati, Ohio.) Perhaps he may try to get employment on a steamboat. He is a good cook, and is handy in any capacity as a house servant. Had on when he left, a dark cassinett coatee, and dark striped cassinett pantaloons, new—he had other clothing. I will give $50 reward if taken in Louisvill; 100 dollars if taken one hundred miles from Louisville in this State, and 150 dollars if taken out of this State, and delivered to me, or secured in any jail so that I can get him again.   WILLIAM BURKE.

Bardstown, Ky., September 3d, 1838.

Up until about 1800, there were a few slaves in northern states. But from the beginning, most slaves were sold in the South. The slaves were forced to work in the fields, on plantations. They were not allowed to talk freely among themselves. So they found special ways to pass messages to each other.

One way was a kind of work song called the *field holler.* One slave would call out a line of a song, then another slave or group would call back, very much like the call and response music in Africa. The slaves used the music to make their hard work a little less boring. These field hollers could also be songs of great sadness.

Many of the white "masters" made the slaves learn the language and customs of white people. Some also taught their slaves Christianity. They thought Christianity would make the slaves more obedient. But it did something else. The new religion gave the slaves hope and helped them through the hardest times.

Often, groups of black people would sneak into the woods at night where they could pray to God in their own way. They could also speak out against the terrible wrongs that were being done to them. Black preachers would give the people hope. The people looked forward to a day when they would be free.

The new religion gave the slaves another way to express their feelings through music. The slaves would sing songs that made them feel good inside and take away some of their pain and anger. These songs might say, "God, I'd rather die and be with you than to be treated like this." The songs had names like "Nobody Knows the Trouble I've Seen" and "Roll, Jordan, Roll."

Religion played an important role in the slaves' everyday lives. Turning to prayer was often their only source of comfort.

They even sang songs that had secret messages about escaping to the North where African Americans were free. One of these songs is called "Steal Away." And spirituals like "Great Day" looked ahead to the great day when the slaves would be freed.

In 1863 Abraham Lincoln signed the Emancipation Proclamation, making
all the slaves free men and women. They did not become truly free
until 1865, at the end of the great Civil War between North and South.

These are members of the 107th Infantry Division, an all-black
military group that fought for the North in the Civil War.

Great Day

Spiritual

Arrangement by Leotha Stanle

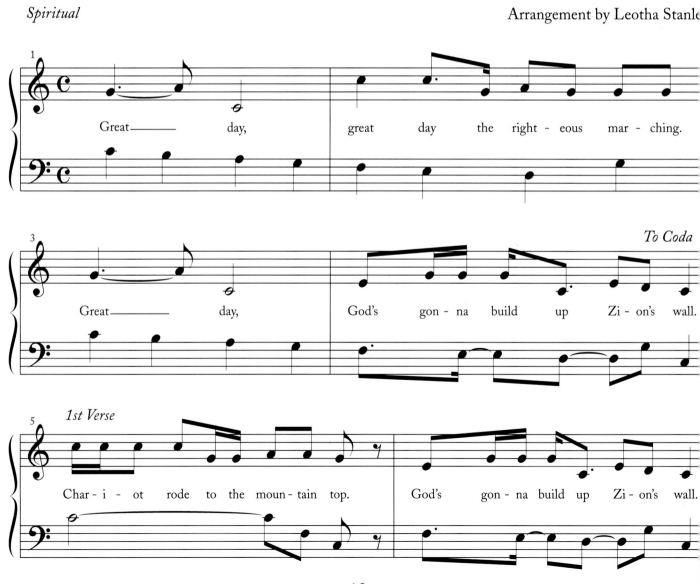

2nd Verse

I was a mourner just like you.
God's gonna build up Zion's wall.
I prayed and prayed til I come through.
God's gonna build up Zion's wall.

3rd Verse

This is the year of jubilee.
God's gonna build up Zion's wall.
When my Lord set His people free.
God's gonna build up Zion's wall.

4th Verse

Don't want no cowards in our band.
God's gonna build up Zion's wall.
We call for valiant hearted men.
God's gonna build up Zion's wall.

BLUES

Have you ever heard someone talk about feeling blue or having the blues? When someone has the blues, that person is feeling sad or is just too tired to feel very happy. That's how blues music got its name.

Blues songs are sung with the same strong feeling as spirituals. In some ways the two types of music sound very much alike. But spirituals are religious songs, and blues music deals with the problems in life that people face every day. Many blues songs tell stories about a woman being bad to a man or a man being bad to a woman.

Here are a few lines from "Slave to the Blues" written by Gertrude "Ma" Rainey in 1926:

You see me ravin', you hear me crying,
Oh Lawd this lonely heart of mine,
Sometimes, I'm grieving from my hat
*   down to my shoes,*
I'm a good-hearted woman that's
*   a slave to the blues.*

Bessie Smith was one of the greatest blues singers of all time.

Gertrude "Ma" Rainey is shown here with her band. Many call her the "mother of the blues."

Like spirituals, the blues can have a sad sound and sad words. But not all blues songs are this way. Some are even funny. Others can calm you down when you're upset. Blues music can make you feel good even when the song is about something sad.

At the end of the Civil War, after the Emancipation Proclamation was signed, African Americans were finally free. But their lives were not easy. They had to work very hard to make a living. And they often had to put up with people who still wanted to treat them badly, just because of the color of their skin.

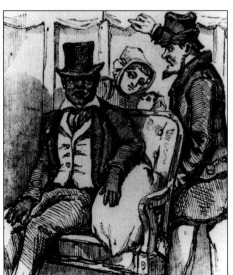

But as hard as life was for most of these former slaves, they were now free. And that meant they were free to try new things with their music.

This engraving shows a black man being kicked out of a railway car for "whites only."

16

For blacks in the South, life still consisted mostly of working long hours in the cotton fields.

Using instruments like guitar and harmonica, African Americans created blues music. Soon the sound of blues music could be heard wherever there was hard work in the fields.

Blues music started in the country. But blues singers wandered from place to place telling stories with their music. They would sing songs with names like "I'm a Po' Boy, 'Long Way from Home."

Soon people who lived and worked in the cities started playing blues music. In places like New Orleans, street peddlers would sell their goods by singing the blues to passersby.

A man sells fruit and vegetables on a city street.

W. C. Handy was the first person to make the blues really popular. He wrote his first blues song in 1912. His most famous song is "St. Louis Blues." Ma Rainey was one of the first to make a living by singing the blues. But in the 1920s and 1930s Bessie Smith became the most famous woman blues singer ever. She made the blues even more popular.

W. C. Handy

Blues musicians came to the North as part of a huge group of black Americans looking for a better way of life in the 1910s and 1920s. In the 1940s a new name was given to a kind of blues music that became very popular. This music was called rhythm and blues or R&B. White singers like Elvis Presley and Jerry Lee Lewis sang music that came out of this style.

Elvis Presley

During the 1950s this type of music was renamed rock and roll. Later, new styles of music, including soul, funk, and Motown also became popular.

But all of these styles started with the music of the blues and another kind of African American music called jazz.

Top R&B performer B. B. King continues to influence today's pop artists.

18

"School Blues"

The "School Blues" takes us along on a trip from kindergarten to grade five, showing us the hardships of elementary school along the way. Making it to sixth grade is a major accomplishment. There is so much homework to do! But after all is said and done, it's a trip that's well worth the effort. – *L. S.*

School Blues

With Feeling (♩. = 72)

Words and Music by Leotha Stanley

When I was in kin-der-gar———ten, my first day at school, didn't know how to read or write,——— or tie my shoes. I passed the first grade. The se-cond grade too. Don't know how I made it, with all that home-work to do. The third grade was

Jazz

Harlem's Apollo Theatre is still a place where many great black musicians perform.

Jazz is music that really deals with what it means to be an American.

Wynton Marsalis, in *Ebony*,
February 1986

Jazz is exciting. Jazz is free. Jazz is music that makes you snap your fingers and tap your feet. And jazz can make you think.

In many ways, jazz music is like an expansion of the blues. But jazz is more complicated in the way it is made up, or composed. It is usually fast in tempo and makes you feel like dancing. Jazz is also a kind of music that people can change while they play it. This is called *improvisation*. Improvisation is an important part of jazz. It allows the musician to put his or her own spirit into a song.

Another important part of jazz is something called *syncopation*. Syncopation has to do with the rhythm of the music. It adds energy to the music.

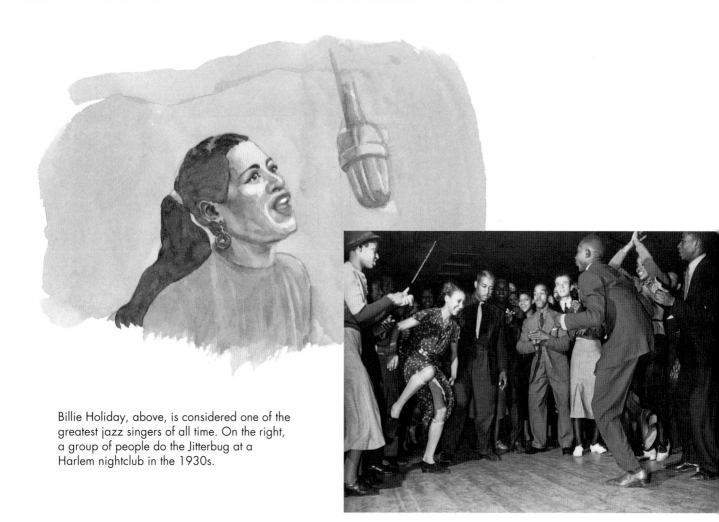

Billie Holiday, above, is considered one of the greatest jazz singers of all time. On the right, a group of people do the Jitterbug at a Harlem nightclub in the 1930s.

Most songs get their rhythm from a regular beat. Syncopation happens when a strong sound is placed not *on* the regular beat but *between* the regular beats. Syncopation helps give jazz its special sound.

In many ways jazz is more about being yourself than any other kind of music. One jazz musician named Chico Freeman said: "To be a jazz musician you have to have a very strong belief in yourself. You have to be true to yourself in ways other people are not. You have to speak with your own voice."

Jazz was born when the African American people started to become freer to be themselves. It helped African Americans show their personal feelings. It gave them another way to talk about the things that happened to them and the way they felt. In spirituals, musicians sing about a life to come. In blues, they sing about this life. In jazz, musicians "talk" about the life of the mind.

A jazz record album from the early 1950s.

24

Beginning in 1915 and through the 1940s, many blacks moved from the country to the cities, where there were more jobs. One city they moved to was New Orleans. Some people say New Orleans is where jazz was born. People heard jazz there for the first time and began to play the music themselves. Before long, the New Orleans jazz style had moved to Chicago and New York. In a very short time, jazz was being heard all over the world.

Jazz was a new musical style that became very popular. But in many ways it was not new at all. Like blues and spirituals, it had its beginnings in the long-ago memories of the Africans who first came to America.

For example, the music of West Africa is known for its unusual rhythms. The strong sound of drums in the background gives the music a lot of feeling and rhythm. Jazz music uses drums in much the same way.

Jazz also uses instruments that often are made to sound like voices. Maybe you have heard the long wail of a saxophone or trumpet that sounds almost like a person crying out.

The Tin Roof Cafe, pictured on this sheet music cover, was a popular New Orleans nightclub in the 1920s. It featured jazz and blues music.

Saxophonist John Coltrane

Some say that a style of piano music called ragtime was the beginning of the jazz style. Ragtime used syncopation to make its sound. In the 1890s, a piano musician named Scott Joplin wrote and played some of the best-known ragtime music. He came to be known as the "king of ragtime." His most famous song is "Maple Leaf Rag."

Scott Joplin

Other styles of African American music, like the blues, also played a big part in giving jazz its sound. Hundreds of African American jazz musicians and artists have become famous. Some of the best known are Duke Ellington, Count Basie, Louis Armstrong, Billie Holiday, Ella Fitzgerald, Miles Davis, Dizzy Gillespie, and John Coltrane. Not only did they help jazz become popular, they never stopped being popular themselves.

The Cotton Club in Harlem launched the careers of many famous jazz musicians.

Duke Ellington

Dizzy Gillespie

Ella Fitzgerald

"Brain Power"

This jazz song is about education and how important it is in our lives. Education is our BRAIN POWER. Without education we are not using all of the power our brains have. Education gets us ready for the real world. That is why it is so important to stay in school and graduate from high school. After all, graduation is our shining hour. — *L. S.*

"A Friend Indeed"

One way to make the world a better place is to help a friend in need. When one person is helped, then that person can help another. A kind word helps a lot when someone is feeling down. If you can notice that a friend needs a boost and you say or do something to make that person smile, then you are truly A FRIEND INDEED. — *L. S.*

Brain Power

Jazz

Words and Music by Leotha Stanley

2nd Verse

In science, I learn how the grass turns green.
I keep the beat in music like a rhythm machine.
I wonder just how much my brain can hold.
Information in and out, the answer's untold.

3rd Verse

After middle school, there's senior high,
Working toward the day when my tassle will fly.
I've learned a whole lot more, I have the basic knowledge.
Diploma in my hand now it's off to college.

1992 by Musical-Lee Yours

Friend Indeed

Swing

Words and Music by Leotha Stanley

Some-times when you're feel-ing— low, you need some-bo-dy— that you know,— to perk you up when you're feel-ing— bad, to make you hap-py when you're feel-ing— sad. If you're an F - R - I - E - N - D friend in need———— I'll be an F - R - I - E - N - D friend in - deed.———— —— Hold your head up— high.——— Keep it to the— sky.— —— Sing a hap-py—— song.——— —— Your wor-ries will be— gone.——— Don't you dare look— down.— —— Don't you wear a— frown.— And soon you will see——— how hap-py you can be.

30

31

GOSPEL

Thomas A. Dorsey

If you can imagine what happens when you mix blues music with the comforting words of spirituals, then you know what gospel music is like. Gospel songs speak of hope, peace, joy, and love. In other words, gospel sends a "good news" message.

Mixing these two different kinds of music was the idea of Thomas A. Dorsey. Mr. Dorsey was a Chicago blues musician who wrote songs and played for great singers like Ma Rainey in the 1920s. He had also

been writing some gospel songs. But after his wife and baby died unexpectedly, he turned all his energy to religion.

But Mr. Dorsey did not leave blues music behind. He took songs he wrote for church and played them to the music of the blues. Some church people were upset because they didn't think blues music should be played in church. But the people who went to the churches loved the new music because it spoke to their hearts. It gave a whole new hand-clapping feeling to church music and drew everyone into the songs.

In gospel music a chorus will often respond to, or answer, the main singer after a line of song. The chorus and singer will go back and forth in this way—just like the call and response music of Africa.

Body movement is another important part of gospel music, just as dance was important in African music. In gospel, the chorus will nearly always clap, tap, sway, or beat tambourines. One of the really wonderful things about gospel is that the audience is stirred by the music. The audience is encouraged to become part of the chorus.

Mr. Dorsey knew this would happen. Call and response is also an important part of some blues songs, and Mr. Dorsey knew the blues and how much people loved it. During his life, he wrote nearly 1,000 songs. His most famous is "Take My Hand, Precious Lord." He also introduced female backup singers to gospel music. Mr. Dorsey has been called "the father of gospel music."

Popular singers like Aretha Franklin, Sam Cooke, and Diana Ross all got their start by singing gospel music. The most famous gospel singer of all time is Mahalia Jackson. Another great gospel singer is Rosetta Tharpe. More recently, gospel artists like Take Six, Edwin Hawkins, the Mighty Clouds of Joy, and the Dixie Hummingbirds have helped bring gospel music to people of all races and religions.

Aretha Franklin

Mahalia Jackson

Mt. Zion Baptist Church Choir, Madison, Wisconsin. Choir director and author Leotha Stanley is seated at the organ.

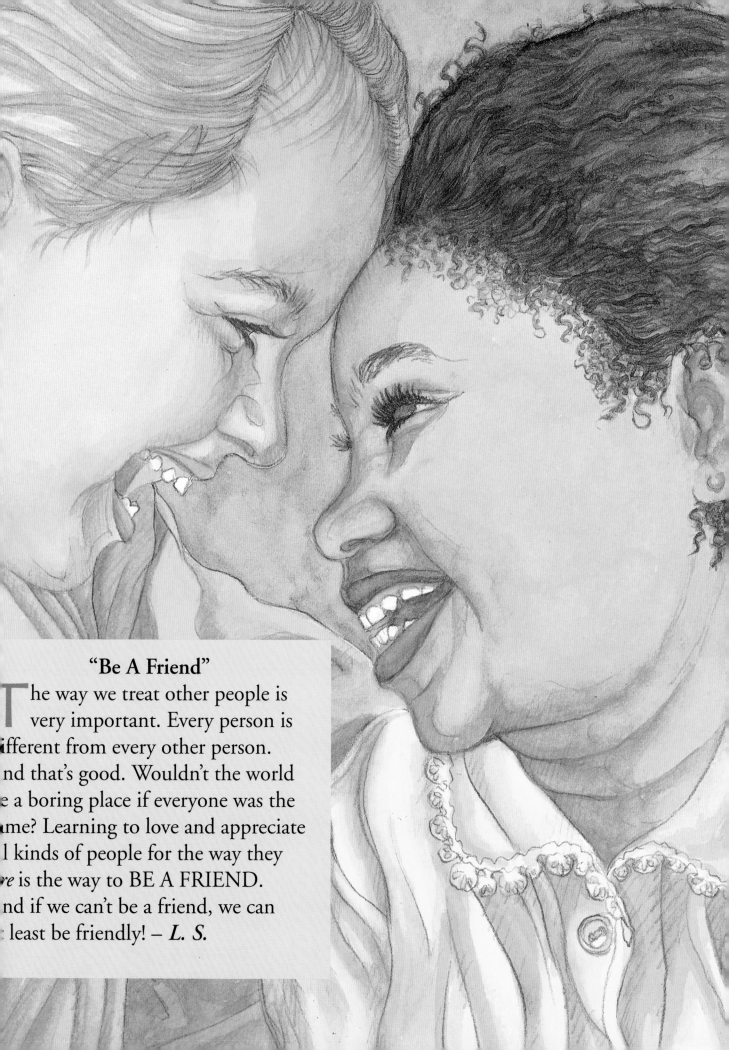

"Be A Friend"

The way we treat other people is very important. Every person is different from every other person. And that's good. Wouldn't the world be a boring place if everyone was the same? Learning to love and appreciate all kinds of people for the way they *are* is the way to BE A FRIEND. And if we can't be a friend, we can at least be friendly! – *L. S.*

Be A Friend

Words and Music by Leotha Stan

Gospel

Take a sis-ter by the hand—— tell a bro-ther yes he can—— find a way to

make a friend—— eve-ry-where.—— Op-en up your hearts to all—— ne-ver let you

love be too small—— al-ways find a way to stand tall—— and be a friend who cares.——

Say what you mean—— and mean what you say.—— E - qual rights for your neigh-bor—— i

To Coda

36

Just Say No

With Feeling

Words and Music by Leotha Stanley

Just say no to drugs.— Give your life a chance.—

—————— You've got to take—

a stand.————

Give your life a chance.————

You've got to take a stand.—

—————— *Rap* Give your life a chance.————

"Just Say No"

No may be one of the hardest words to say. Some of our biggest problems might come when we want to say no but we say yes to please someone. For instance, drugs are very bad for us, and the people who sell and use drugs are bad for us also. Getting high on *hugs* is a better choice. Take a stand for the good things in life. To drugs and the people who use them, JUST SAY NO. – *L. S.*

Rap

Rap uses fast-talking words spoken with rhythm to a beat. Rap is one of the most popular forms of music with young people today. It is very cool, very hip, and very happening. But even rap had its beginnings a long time ago.

One of Africa's great traditions is storytelling through music. For hundreds of years, people shared news, gossip, and even insults in song. Men and women called *praise-singers* made up poems and songs about the great deeds of their leaders. Praise-singing is still done in Africa today.

This custom of telling stories through poems and songs set to music found its way into the storytelling traditions of the old South. Then it found its way into the music of the blues. Later it became part of the patter of be-bop jazz and today's rap.

Rap music as we know it today started here in the late 1970s as dance music. It became really popular in the 1980s. Disc jockeys helped to start this style of music by making new beats and sounds while

spinning records. Early rap in America was similar to a form of black music called *toasting*, which began in Jamaica in the 1960s as an offshoot of the popular reggae music.

In the United States, DJ Kool Herc was one of the first to start "rapping" or talking to the beat of the music he was playing. DJ Grandmaster Flash used a drum machine with parts of other records to make a whole new sound of his own. Musicians like Run D.M.C., L L Cool J, and M. C. Hammer helped rap become popular with all groups of young people.

Artists like Queen Latifah, MC Lyte, and Salt-N-Pepa opened the way for women in rap music.

Many singers use rap to send a strong message to an audience. Some people have been upset by rap because some singers use bad words or send bad messages. But many singers use rap to send good messages and to encourage young people to do the right thing.

Rap artists (top to bottom) L L Cool J, Queen Latifah, and MC Lyte.

"We Shall Overcome"

"Someday" isn't soon enough to overcome hatred and prejudice. We must do it today — NOW — immediately. It starts with each one of us and then we can pass it on. If you believe this in your heart, then you can convince more people to get involved in ending discrimination and injustice. WE SHALL OVERCOME sooner than someday. Let's try it today! – *L. S.*

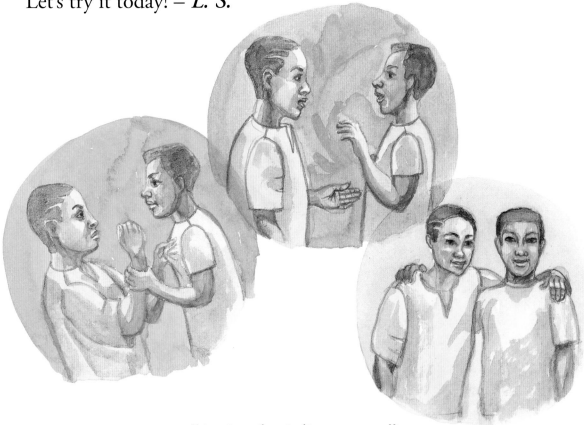

"Attitude Adjustment"

Some of us have short fuses. When we are angry, it may take only a short while for us to explode. A good attitude can help us get through the times when we are disappointed with friends, parents, or teachers. If we adjust our attitudes, we can avoid fights or other kinds of trouble. We can move forward in life by reacting with thought and not anger, but only if we can ADJUST OUR ATTITUDE. – *L. S.*

We Shall Overcome

Arrangement by Leotha Stanley

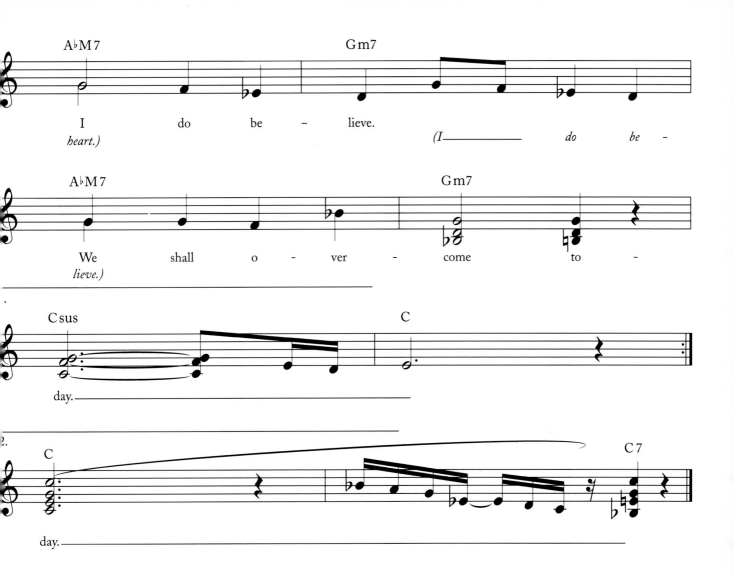

I do be - lieve.
heart.)   (I⎯⎯⎯ do be -

We shall o - ver - come to -
lieve.)

day.

day.

2nd Verse

Let's all get together, it's the way it should be.
Respect for one another like a family.
Brothers and sisters have to be as one,
Fighting for justice, to get the job done!

3rd Verse

We're all different down here under the sun.
We don't have to fight, we can simply have fun.
So, put down your knife, and put down your gun.
Black, White, Red, Yellow, We Shall Overcome!

Attitude Adjustment

Words and Music by Leotha Stan[...]

We___ all___ need___ an at - ti - tude___ ad - just - ment. We___ all___ need___ an at - ti - tude___ ad - just - ment. at - ti - tude___ ad - just - ment. Some___

times I think I'm shrewd and some - times I think I'm rude.

Look - ing for a con - ver - sa - tion where I can in - trude. Then I

looked in the mir - ror and I said, "HEY DUDE."

What you need to do is ad - just your at - ti - tude. Just fine___ tune the___

2nd Verse

I said, "Teacher understand me, that's all I'm looking for.
Treat me like a person and I won't think you're a bore."
Then I worked a little harder, increased my aptitude.
We both came out ahead because we changed our ATTITUDE.
(Refrain, Measure 14 then Verse 3)

3rd Verse

I really thought it over, and found it plain to see.
How I react to what you do is certainly the key.
So, if you ever do me wrong, I won't come unglued.
I'll count to ten and say why not ADJUST MY ATTITUDE!
(Refrain, Measure 14, Refrain then Coda)

The music goes on . . .

From spirituals to blues, from jazz to gospel to rap, African American music is a large part of America's most loved and popular music. And all of these styles continue to be popular even after other styles have come and gone.

Why do we like African American music so much? And why is it so important to American music? Does it talk to you? Does it help you express what you feel, or what you think? Maybe you should put a tape on your player and answer those questions for yourself.